AF290380

Jacob El Hanani

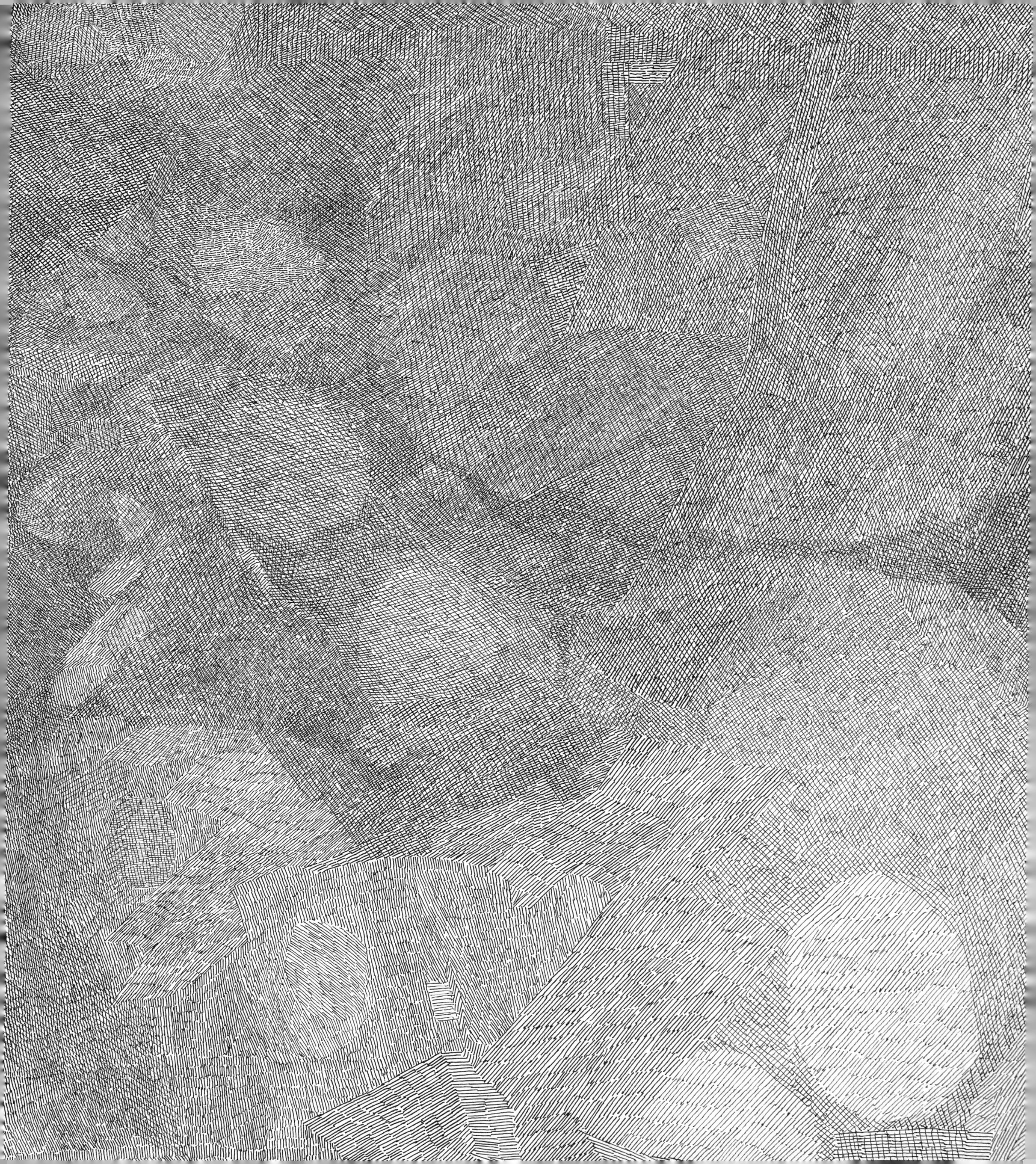

Jacob El Hanani

Recent Works on Canvas

Essay by
ADAM KIRSCH

ACQUAVELLA

Rizzoli
NEW YORK

This publication accompanies the exhibition

Jacob El Hanani
Recent Works on Canvas

ON VIEW
Acquavella Galleries
May 5 – June 18, 2021

ACQUAVELLA

18 East Seventy-Ninth Street
New York, NY 10075

LIBRARY OF CONGRESS CONTROL NUMBER
2021931115

ISBN
978–0–8478–6914–5

DISTRIBUTION
Rizzoli International Publications, Inc.
300 Park Avenue South
New York, NY 10010
www.rizzoliusa.com

DESIGN
HvADesign, NYC

PRINT
Phoenix Group, Philadelphia, PA

FRONTISPIECE
*Without Form and Void
(Tohu Va-vohu)* [detail], 2018
Ink on gessoed canvas
50 × 50 inches

PAGE 7
*The Horizontal Hebrew
Alphabet* [detail], 2019
Ink on gessoed canvas
24 × 30 inches

*"It is a personal challenge
to bring drawing to
the extreme
and see how far my eyes
and fingers can go."*

—JACOB EL HANANI

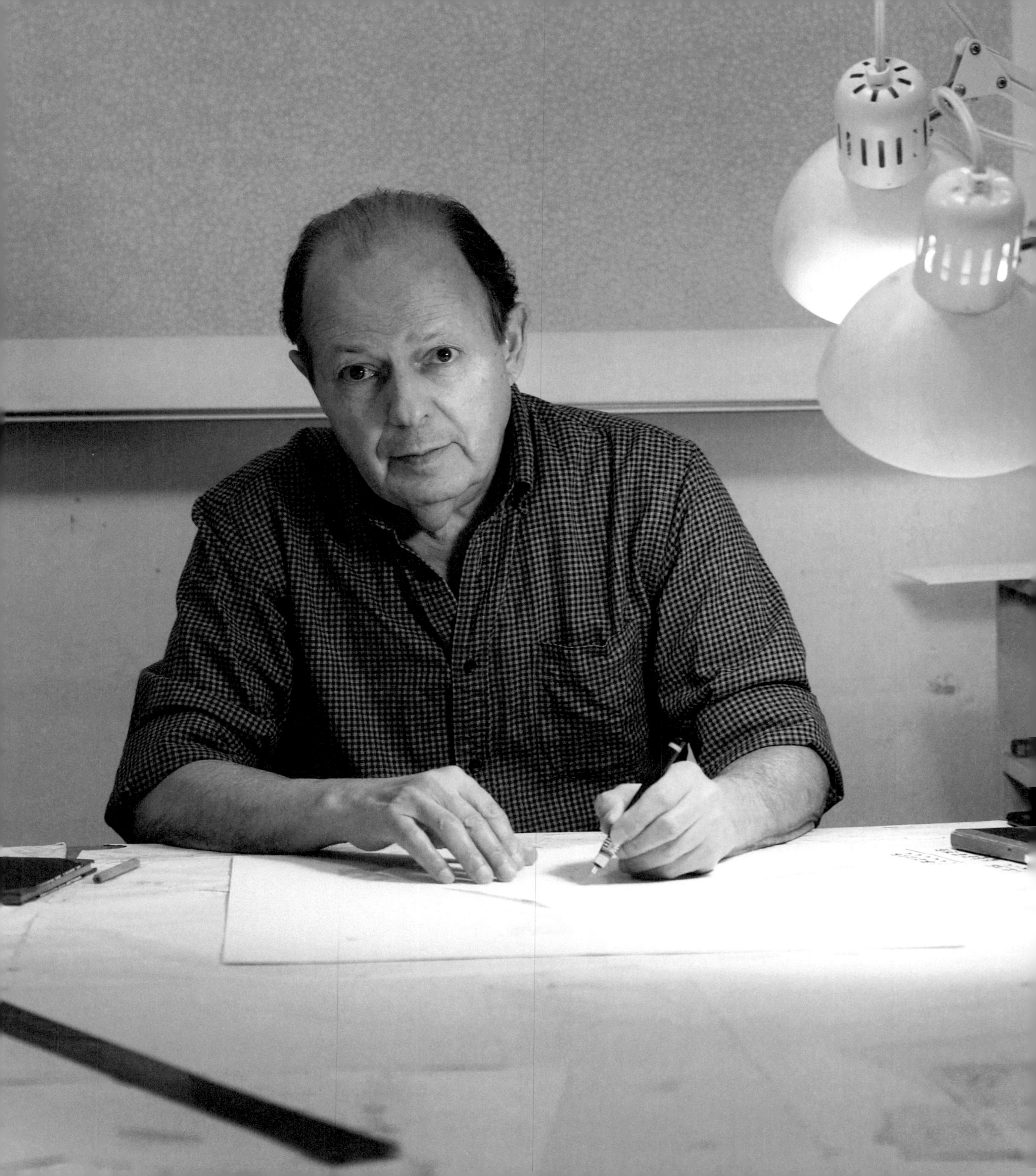

Foreword

ELEANOR ACQUAVELLA

We are delighted to present this exhibition of new works on canvas by Jacob El Hanani, our third exhibition dedicated to the artist at the gallery. For five decades, Jacob has produced painstakingly detailed pen-and ink drawings composed of countless microscopic marks woven into all-over abstractions. Often called "the grandfather of micro-drawing," he makes works that need to be seen up close to appreciate their nearly unfathomable level of detail.

Jacob's drawings employ a range of forms—from minuscule linear strokes and tiny circles to scripted letters of the Hebrew alphabet—which are fluidly strung into evocative patterns. Despite their apparent abstraction, his drawings are often suggestive of atmospheric land-scapes, topographical maps, and carefully woven textiles. Layered with references, Jacob's drawings reflect varied cultural, historical, and personal influences. Born in Casablanca, Morocco in 1947, he was raised in Israel and studied art in Tel Aviv and Paris before moving to New York City in the early 1970s. While his drawings are rooted in the ancient Hebrew tradition of micrography, he fuses this spiritual tradition with a contemporary Minimalist sensibility. When he arrived in New York, Minimalism was at the height of its influence and left an indelible impression on the artist, inspiring his own, highly detailed approach to abstraction.

Jacob's process is exacting, slow, and unforgiving; his elaborate drawings are achieved through extraordinary self-discipline. Since settling into his Soho studio in the early 1970s, where he still lives and works today, Jacob has been accustomed to working long days, his studio a quiet, focused respite from the bustle of the city. With the disruptions of the past year, Jacob has spent even more time in his studio, enabling him to produce this remarkable body of new work. In these new canvases, he has been able to achieve an exceptional level of detail, challenging himself to create very fine, intricate works, often on a larger scale.

Working without a magnifying glass in brief stints in order to rest his eyes and hone his sight, his drawings take months or even years to complete, marking the passage of time and the artist's focus and endurance. The deliberate slowness of his work strikes a counterpoint to the fast-paced tempo of today's world; his images require more than a few seconds of our attention for us to marvel at their complexity and comprehend the process of their creation. They need to be seen up close and in person, rather than through an online platform or reproduction.

We hope that you will be able to visit this exhibition of Jacob's work. The show will be on view concurrently with our loan exhibition, *Eva Hesse / Hannah Wilke: Erotic Abstraction*, which was postponed from the spring of 2020. For their help in making this exhibition and publication possible, we would like to thank John Andrew and Emily Crowley at the gallery, photographer Kent Pell, graphic designer Henk van Assen and his team at HvADesign, Keith Harrington and Phoenix Lithographing, and Ellen Cohen and Charles Miers at Rizzoli. Our gratitude goes to the writer and poet Adam Kirsch for his insightful essay published in this book, which elegantly explores Jacob's work in the context of Jewish history, language, and tradition. But above all, we would like to thank Jacob for making these works and for letting us share them with the public.

Jacob El Hanani
Black Fire on White Fire

ADAM KIRSCH

The Talmud teaches that the original Torah, the one God gave to Moses on Mount Sinai, was "written in black fire on white fire." Today we might call it virtual—pure information, independent of any physical medium. If so, then the Torah scrolls written by generation after generation of Jewish scribes are only attempts to trap that fiery text in parchment and ink.

But scripture can conceal as much of God's meaning as they reveal. The Torah has seventy faces, according to a famous rabbinic saying, and not all of them can be glimpsed simply by reading the words. Jewish mysticism has long tried to draw meaning from permutations of the Torah's individual letters, believing that the Hebrew alphabet pre-existed the universe. "Two thousand years before the creation of the world, the Creator gazed into the letters and played with them," says the Zohar, the medieval Spanish text that is the foundation of Kabbalah.

Even the shapes of the letters hold secret meanings. The first word in Genesis is *bereshit*, "in the beginning": why, mystics have wondered, did God choose to begin the Torah with the letter *bet*, which, like its English equivalent "B," is the second letter in the alphabet? Why not start with the first letter, *aleph*? A homiletical interpretation or Midrash from the 5th century C.E. explains that the letter was chosen because of its form: "Just as the *bet* is closed on all sides and open in front, so we have no right to inquire what is below, what is above, what is behind, but only from the day that the world was created and thereafter."

Jacob El Hanani often uses Hebrew letters in his work, though he is neither a mystic nor a scribe. His abstract drawings, which conjure wavering networks and textures through the accretion of minute, hand-drawn lines, situate him in the context of minimalism, the art movement that was flourishing in New York when he moved there in 1974. El Hanani was among the artists drawn to Soho by the availability of cheap lofts, where they could work and (illegally) live. His studio was, and still is, on lower Broadway. A few blocks away on Prince Street, Paula Cooper Gallery was showing work by the minimalist masters Donald Judd and Sol LeWitt, who lived in the area. "The '60s were clutter. The '70s are very empty," said Andy Warhol in his *The Philosophy of Andy Warhol*, published in 1975.

But El Hanani discovered that it is possible to maintain emptiness while suffusing it with marks and meanings—and it was Jewish tradition that showed him the way. While Jewish themes and titles appear in the work of other minimalists like Mark Rothko and Barnett Newman, El Hanani's upbringing gives him access to a tradition that runs deeper than allusion. He was born in Casablanca, Morocco, in 1947, into a Jewish community that had ancient roots—there have been Jews in the country since Roman times—but lived modern, urban, Francophone lives.

El Hanani's family moved to Israel in 1953, part of a mass migration that reduced Morocco's Jewish population from some 250,000 in 1948 to just 2,000 today. His upbringing gave him a fluency in Jewish texts and ideas that continues to inform his work, even though he has now lived in New York twice as long as he lived in Israel.

Take *Circle-Maker (Honi Hame'aggel)* (2019–20), one of his most ambitious and profound works, completed last year. From a distance, the canvas looks like a wash of grays, delicately transitioning between shades like patches of cloudy sky. Seen more closely, it reveals itself as an enormously complex mesh of tiny circles. Hand-drawn, like all of El Hanani's work, these circles aren't perfectly round—not ball-bearings from a machine but packed cells seen under a microscope.

The title, however, opens up a new, specifically Jewish dimension of meaning. Honi Hame'aggel—in English, Honi the Circle-Drawer—is the subject of a theologically provocative story in the Talmud. During a serious drought, Honi issued a challenge to God: drawing a circle around himself in the dirt, he declared, "I take an oath by Your great name that I will not move from here until You have mercy upon Your children." When a little rain began to fall, Honi complained that God wasn't sending enough; when the rain grew dangerously strong, he complained that it was too much. Finally, God got it right and the rain continued until Honi told God to stop.

The Talmud itself isn't quite sure what to make of this story. Issuing ultimatums to God is hardly an expression of the humility and piety that Judaism prizes; yet the fact remains that God did bow to Honi's demand. As the head of the Jewish court complained, "Were you not Honi, I would have decreed that you be ostracized, but what can I do to you? You nag God and He does your bidding, like a son who nags his father."

What does El Hanani mean by titling his own circle drawing after Honi? Is it a witty allusion, one that only quite learned Jews are likely to understand? Or is there a deeper similarity between the ancient sage and the modern artist, whose practice also rests on audacity, persistence and faith? If El Hanani draws countless circles while Honi only had to make one, perhaps it's a sign that God has become exponentially harder to reach. Such theological resonances are inescapable in much of El Hanani's work, making it as challenging to the mind as it is to the eye.

Like many artists, El Hanani had to distance himself from home and tradition before he discovered how to put them to use. When he came to America in 1974, after studying at Tel Aviv's Avni Institute for Art and Design and the École des Beaux Arts in Paris, his work was figurative. (He is still a talented caricaturist, able to capture faces on the fly with a few strokes.) It was in New York that El Hanani developed what I have heard him call his *chiddush*—the word used by Talmudic scholars to refer to a novel textual interpretation, a distinctively personal contribution to tradition.

In El Hanani's case, this was a unique approach to abstraction that allows him to reconcile terms usually seen as opposites—modern and ancient, concept and practice, inscription and design. This determination to transcend binaries is perhaps the centrally Jewish impulse in El Hanani's work. Kabbalah is paradoxical through and through, as every mysticism must be when it tries to capture the ineffable in words; and its most important paradox is that *ayin*, emptiness, gave rise to *yesh*, being. If the Kabbalists could have pictured that process, it might have looked like an El Hanani drawing: a seething space made of black fire on white fire.

Take *Tehilim* (1978–81), one of El Hanani's biggest (50 inches by 50 inches) and most intricate works, which is in the collection of The Metropolitan Museum of Art. Its countless fine lines appear from a distance as a dark gray mist in which lighter gray patches seem to be emerging, struggling to coalesce into a horizontal band across the middle third of the canvas. Viewed through the lens of minimalism, *Tehilim* can be seen as El Hanani's response to Rothko; viewed through a biblical lens, it could be an illustration of Genesis 1:6: "Let there be a firmament in the midst of the waters, and let it divide the waters from the waters." The title of the work points in a biblical direction: Tehilim is the Hebrew name of the Book of Psalms, a collection of 150 poems that praise God. Perhaps the drawing too is a work of praise, building meaning through the repetition of lines in the same way that a pious Jew or Christian recites the Psalms again and again in daily prayer.

In some of El Hanani's most movingly austere new work, the building blocks for larger patterns are Hebrew letters themselves, rendered almost illegibly minute. In *The Horizontal Hebrew Alphabet* (2019), they are used to create a stack of horizontal bands that gradually shift from dense and dark at the bottom of the canvas to sparse and light at the top. If the elements used to build the image were dots or random marks, the work would appear purely graphic, a study in contrasting tones and textures.

By using Hebrew letters, however, El Hanani places the work into conversation with texts as well as images. "Read" from top to bottom, *The Horizontal Hebrew Alphabet* might evoke the account of Creation in Genesis, where God separates the layers of the world

Jacob El Hanani | *Tehilim*, 1978–81 | Ink on canvas | 50 × 50 inches
The Metropolitan Museum of Art, New York; Gift of Syril and Leonard Rubin, 1983

Mark Rothko | *No. 5*, 1964 | Oil, acrylic, and mixed media on canvas | $81^{3}/_{16} \times 77^{1}/_{16}$ inches
National Gallery of Art, Washington, D.C.; Gift of the Mark Rothko Foundation, Inc.

according to their density—sky, ocean, land. Read from bottom to top, it could be a Kabbalistic image, illustrating the *sefirot* or stages by which the Godhead transitions from the incomprehensible and infinite *Ein Sof* to the *Shekhinah*, the divine presence that watches over this world.

A similar gradation from dark to light appears in *The Hebrew Barb Wire* (2018), but here the shades are built up from letters joined in long, jagged braids. Once again, El Hanani uses letters to create an image that has multiple "readings": barbed wire can suggest both protection or imprisonment, an army base or a concentration camp. This ambivalence toward Hebrew and everything it represents lies at the heart of modern Jewish identity. No wonder the American Jewish poet Karl Shapiro uses the same imagery as El Hanani in his 1954 poem: "The chosen letters bristle like barbed wire / That hedge the flesh of man, / Twisting and tightening the book that warns."

Whether he is using letters or lines, El Hanani consciously situates his work within the long history of Jewish micrography. In the middle ages, Jewish scribes began to decorate biblical manuscripts with images and designs made of very small Hebrew letters. The way they used the technique mirrored the larger visual cultures in which they were embedded. Ashkenazi scribes in Christian Europe, where representational art was used for sacred purposes, turned strings of letters into the outlines of animals and plants. Sephardic scribes, living in Islamic cultures where representation was taboo, used letters to create aniconic patterns and designs. As a Moroccan Jewish abstractionist, then, El Hanani belongs to an old tradition.

Judaism has always had a tense relationship with visual representation, starting with the Second Commandment: "Thou shalt not make unto thee any graven image, or any likeness of anything that is in heaven above, or in the earth beneath, or that in the water under the earth." In context, this is clearly an expansion of the First Commandment, "Thou shalt have no other gods before me," meant to forbid the worship of idols. By discouraging visual representation in general, however, the commandment helped to turn Jewish imagination into other channels. The creation and analysis of texts became for Judaism what building cathedrals and painting altarpieces were for Christianity—the grandest and most memorable works of faith.

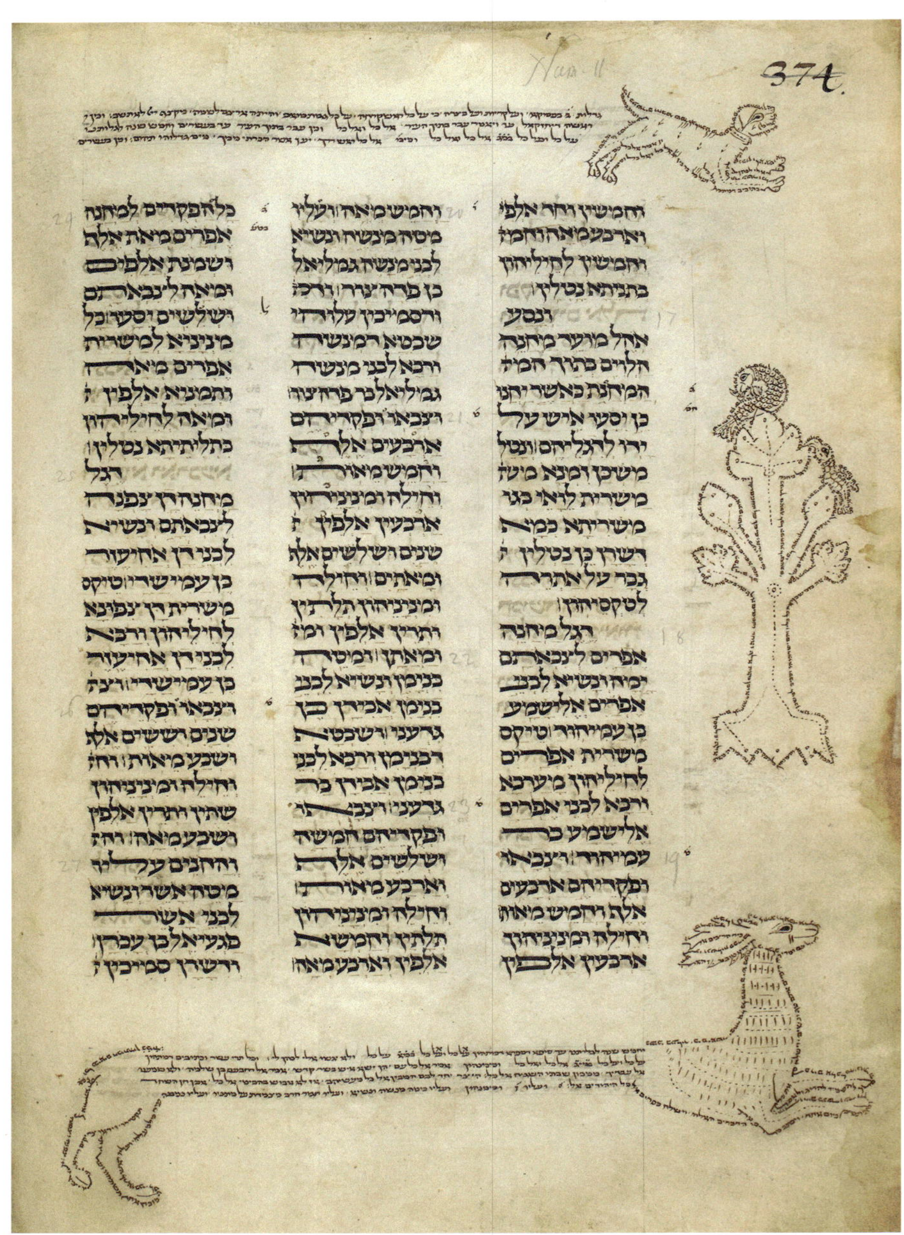

Page from *The Yonah Pentateuch: Pentateuch with prophetical readings*
Created by Baruch (scribe), c. 14th century CE
British Library (MS 21160)

Micrography offered an ingenious way to smuggle image-making back into Judaism, by merging image and text. The words of the Bible itself were sacrosanct, but the scholarly annotations known as the Masorah were fair game, and scribes twisted them into all kinds of figures. In some cases, the words themselves are almost illegible; like the letters in El Hanani's work, they have become more medium than message.

Like those scribes, too, El Hanani's artistic practice resembles a devotional act. It is crucial to the effect and meaning of his work that all his inscriptions are made by hand, using pen and ink on paper or canvas. For more than 40 years, he has worked eight, ten, twelve hours a day, taking breaks every ten minutes to spare his eyesight—he uses no artificial magnification. A Torah scroll contains more than 300,000 letters and usually takes 18 months to write; *Tehilim* took El Hanani twice that long.

El Hanani has stuck to his self-imposed discipline even though all worldly incentives argue against it. He can produce only a few drawings a year; to guard his working time, he finds ways to hold the world at bay. He must be one of the last New Yorkers who does not use a computer or have an email address, much less a social media presence. He still lives and works in the same loft he moved into 46 years ago.

Philosophically, too, El Hanani has quietly defied his times. When he began to chart his artistic course in the 1970s, conceptualism and minimalism were insisting on the separation of idea from execution. Once an artist had the idea for a work, it didn't matter who turned it into a physical object: Warhol's screenprints and Judd's boxes could be produced by anonymous craftsmen, like the apprentices in the atelier of a Renaissance master. As LeWitt wrote in 1967, "The idea becomes a machine that makes the art."

LeWitt is one of the clearest influences on El Hanani, but the artists diverge decisively. LeWitt's wall drawings can be, and have been, made by anyone who follows the artist's instructions. Sometimes those instructions are highly constraining, while in other works they are provocatively minimal: the instructions for *Wall Drawing 86* read simply, "Ten thousand lines about ten inches long, covering the wall 22 23 evenly." This is a kind of algorithm, and the image that results is appropriately mechanical, with straight edges and precise angles. In *Broken Lines* (2019), by contrast, the thousands of line segments are jauntily idiosyncratic—less a mechanical blueprint than a box of matches spilled on the ground. The effect, as in all of El Hanani's work, is totally abstract yet also deeply personal: this particular energy couldn't be generated by any other hand.

Ironically, the postmodernist removal of the artist from the artwork can also be understood as a return of premodern ideas about design and execution, particularly in a Jewish context. According to Jewish law, every adult man is obligated to write a Torah scroll at least once in his lifetime; in practice, the task is delegated to a professional scribe or *sofer*. And a *sofer* works in much the same way as the executor of a LeWitt wall drawing, following strict rules that leave minimal room for individual interpretation. A Torah scroll must be written with black ink made of gall nuts, on parchment made from the skin of a kosher animal, using a quill or reed pen (not an iron one, since iron is used to make weapons). The scribe incises a straight line as a guide before drawing the letters, whose forms are exactly prescribed.

Even deviations from the rule follow a rule. For instance, the Song of the Sea in Exodus 15:1-18, sung by the Israelites after they crossed the Red Sea, is laid out in a distinctive pattern that is the same in every Torah scroll. For this reason, David Stern points out in his 2018 book *The Jewish Bible: A Material History*, it's exceptionally hard to establish the provenance of a Torah scroll, since they look the same in every time and place.

If LeWitt used premodern methods for postmodern ends, however, El Hanani keeps faith with modernism's heroic efforts and baffled quests. Like Jackson Pollock's action paintings, El Hanani's drawings are records of a process as much as they are executions of a design. But in this case the action has been pared down and etherealized—not stalking the canvas and spurting paint onto it, but coaxing a form into being with patient, controlled strokes. And while both processes lead to abstraction, their moods are very different: Pollock's work seems to angrily reject representation, while El Hanani's is wistful for it. It is the difference, perhaps, between a painting that fails to become an image and a drawing that fails to become a text.

The idea of a scribe who, like El Hanani, sets to work every day but never produces the same text twice—or never produces a legible text at all—would have appealed to Franz Kafka, another important reference point for this artist. Kafka's great theme is the agony of failed communication—the sense of listening for crucial words that will never be heard. In "An Imperial Message," a microstory first published in a Prague Jewish magazine in 1919, Kafka addresses the reader directly: "The emperor—it is said—sent to you, the one apart, the wretched subject, the tiny shadow that fled far, far from the imperial sun, precisely to you he sent a message from his deathbed." But the messenger carrying his words has so far to travel, so many obstacles to overcome, that it would take him thousands of years to arrive. All you can do is "sit at your window and dream of that message," knowing you will never receive it.

If the "you" of Kafka's story were given ink, paper, and endless time, perhaps he or she would produce drawings like El Hanani's, using the instruments of writing to create something intricate and illegible. In El Hanani's work, that illegibility marks another point where modernism and Jewishness intersect. Even when they have titles like *Gauze* or *Basket with White Space*, to name two recent examples, his drawings do not actually represent gauze or a basket. And while some of his more geometrical drawings evoke cityscapes, road maps or graphs, they are never actually rectilinear—as El Hanani emphasizes in his "Mondrian series," which turn Mondrian's bold grids into idiosyncratic tiling.

But like the best abstractions, or like music, El Hanani's drawings seem to communicate without representing. Perhaps seeing them this way is no more than a kind of pareidolia, the name psychologists give to the human tendency to perceive faces in inanimate objects, like the man in the moon. But that tendency is apparently ineradicable, and it has deep evolutionary roots. Babies instinctively focus on faces even before knowing what they are, because establishing a face-to-face relationship with adults is indispensable if they are to be fed and cared for. The French Jewish philosopher Emmanuel Levinas believed that this kind of face-to-face encounter was the basis of all morality: "The face is what you cannot kill, or at least that whose meaning consists in saying: 'thou shalt not kill.'"

But not all faces look like faces. Nachman of Bratslav, a late-eighteenth-century Hasidic rabbi and storyteller, told a tale called "The Humble King," in which a wise man is dispatched to a remote land to paint a portrait of its ruler, who has never been seen. Even when the wise man is brought into the royal chamber, the king sits behind a curtain to hide himself. But it turns out that the king is so humble that he can't stand to hear himself praised, so when the sage starts to sing his praises, he begins to shrink:

> *Because of the sage's great praise, extolling and magnifying him, the king reached the utmost humility and smallness until he became literally nothing. He could not contain himself, and he threw aside the veil to see who this wise man was that knew and understood all this. His face was revealed, and the sage saw it and brought his portrait back.*

Of course, the humble king is God, and as a Kabbalist, Nachman knew that God must be described by paradoxes. Only when the king has become nothing does he appear; only when there is no face to portray can his portrait be made. What would that portrait look like, and how long would it take to draw it? Would it be made by patiently accumulating lines, or circles, or Hebrew letters? One thing seems likely: as with a work by Jacob El Hanani, you could look at it for a long time without perceiving an image, but when you turned away you would feel you had been shown something real.

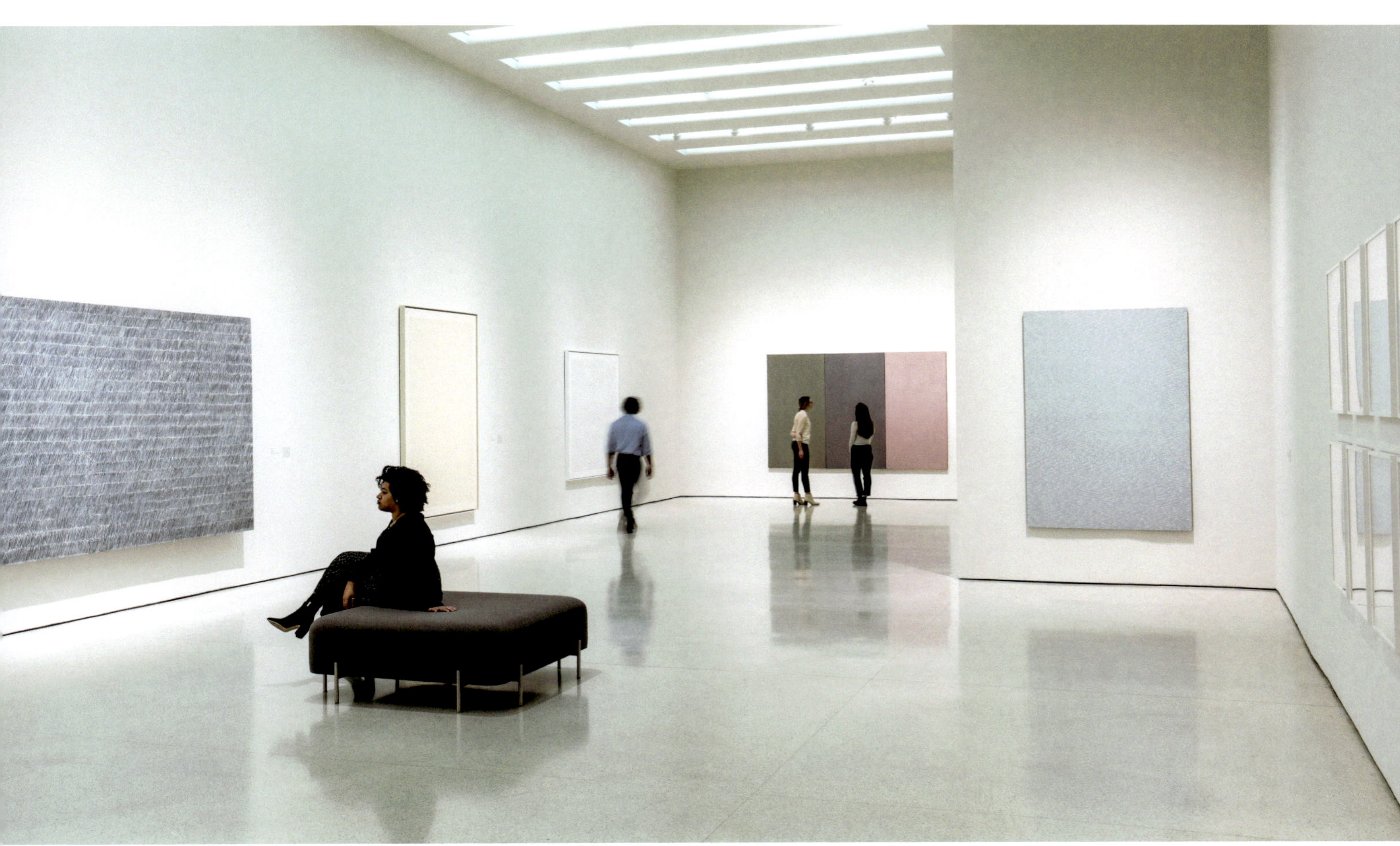

Installation view, *Marking Time: Process in Minimal Abstraction*, December 18, 2019–March 14, 2021, Solomon R. Guggenheim Museum, New York. Works by Park Seo-Bo, Chryssa, Jacob El Hanani, Brice Marden, Roman Opalka, and Zarina on view, left to right.

Works in Exhibition

All works are shown in full, followed by
a detail of the work reproduced at actual size

PLATE 1
The Hebrew Barb Wire, 2018
Ink on gessoed canvas
20 × 20 inches

Detail following

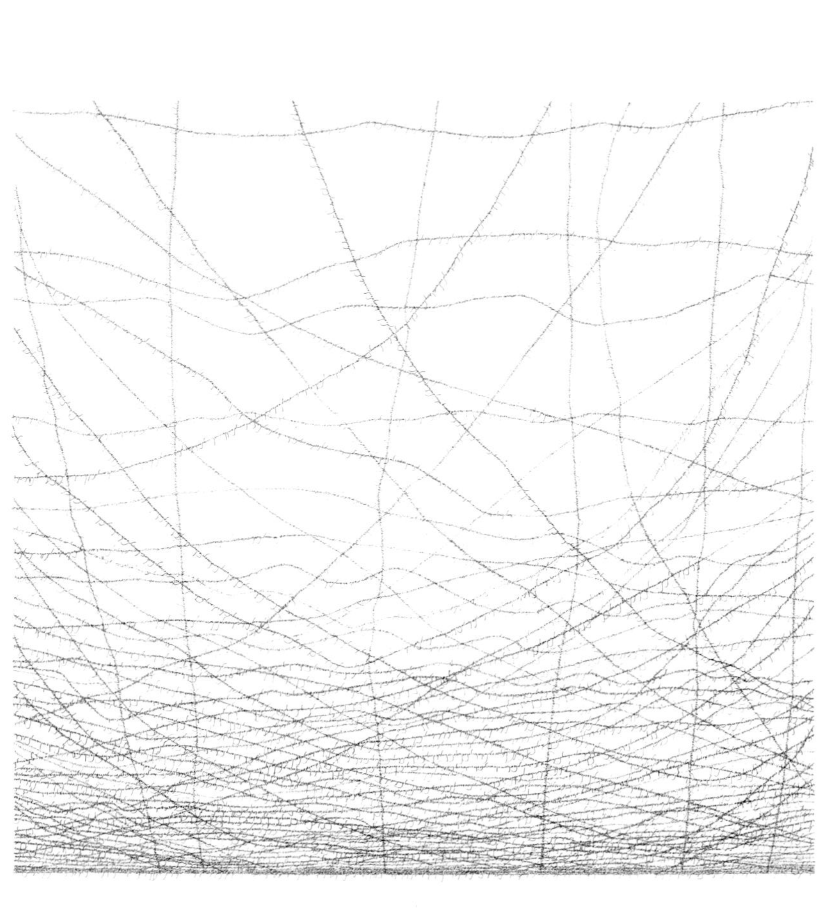

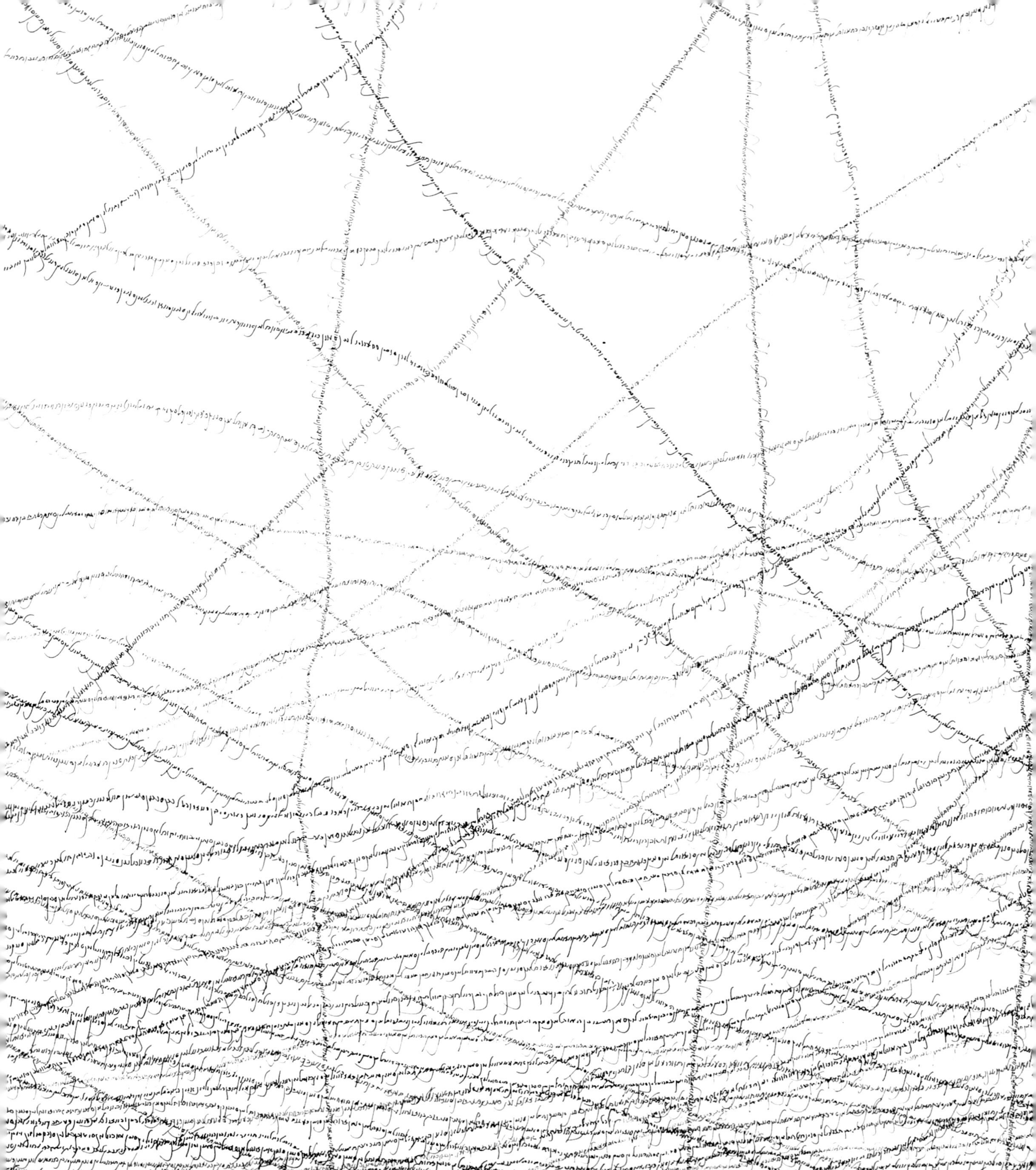

PLATE 2
Diminutive Hebrew Alphabet, 2019
Ink on gessoed canvas
20 × 20 inches

Detail following

PLATE 3
The Horizontal Hebrew Alphabet, 2019
Ink on gessoed canvas
24 × 30 inches

Detail following

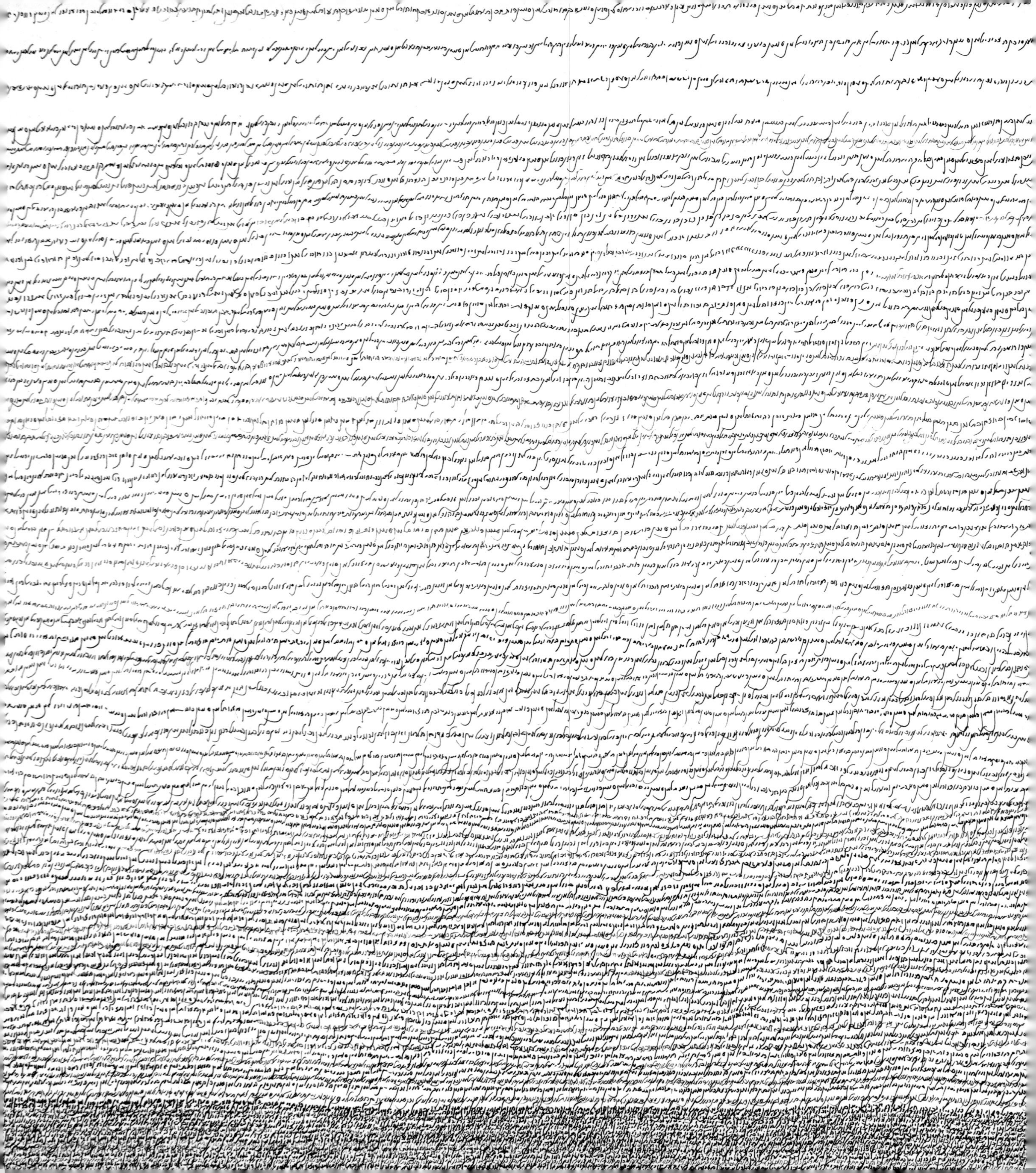

PLATE 4
Circle Maker (Honi Ham'eaggel), 2019–20
Ink on gessoed canvas
50 × 50 inches

Detail following

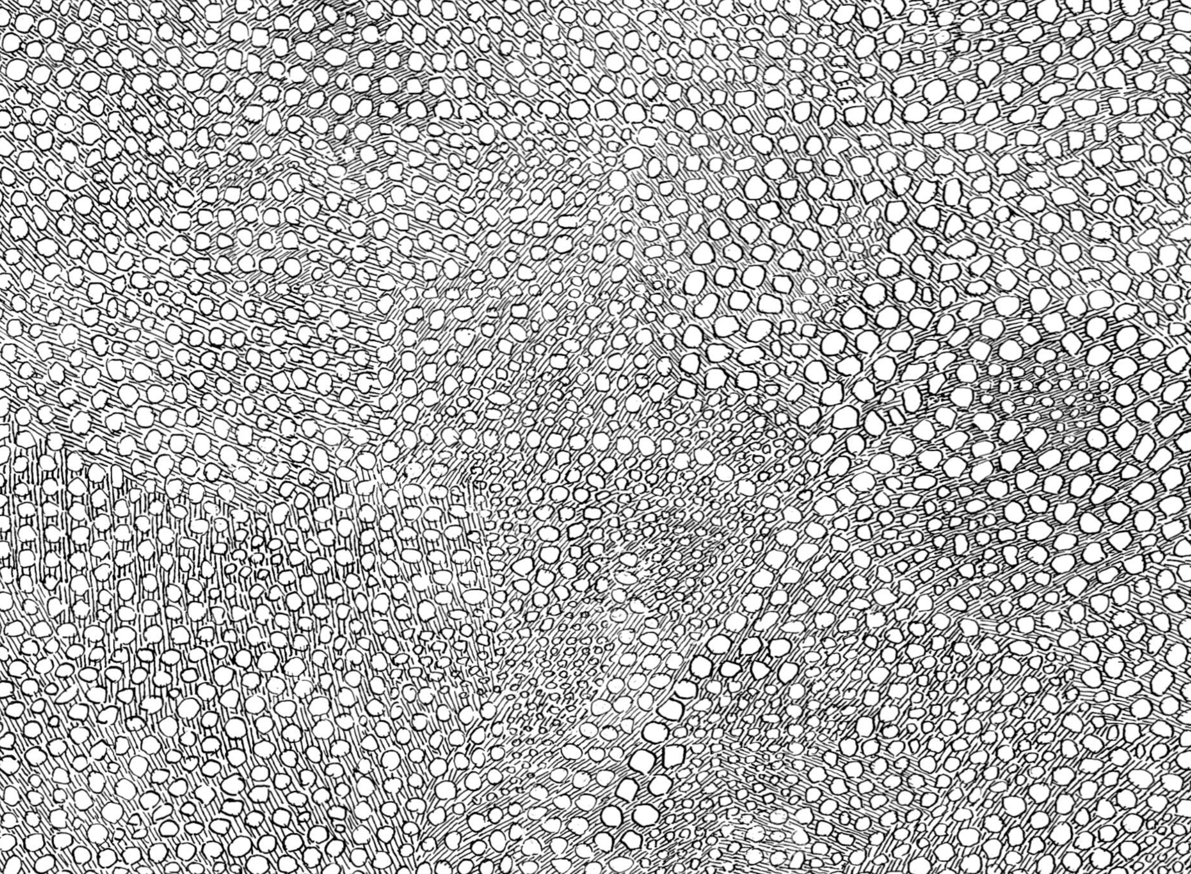

PLATE 5
Horizontal Linescape, 2018
Ink on gessoed canvas
24 × 48 inches

Detail following

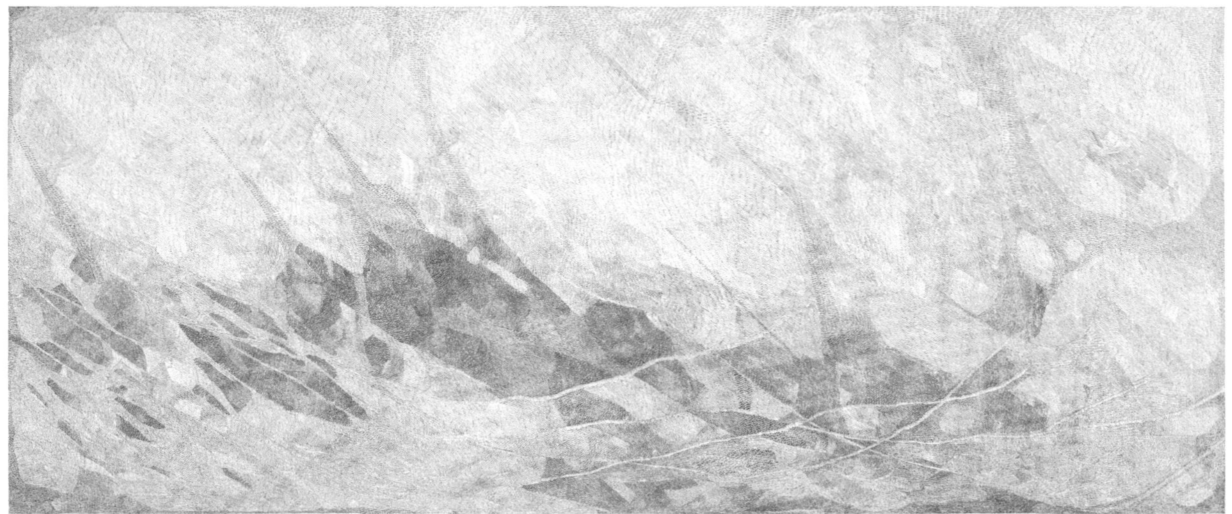

PLATE 6
Dense Circles, 2020
Ink on gessoed canvas
18 × 18 inches

Detail following

PLATE 7
Vertical Dot Linescape, 2019
Ink on gessoed canvas
36 × 36 inches

Detail following

Hebrew Alphabet, 2019
Ink on gessoed canvas
36 × 36 inches

Detail following

PLATE 9
Gauze, 2020
Ink on gessoed canvas
38 × 38 inches

Detail following

PLATE 10
Purple Linescape, 2020
Ink on gessoed canvas
50 × 50 inches

Detail following

PLATE 11
*Without Form and Void
(Tohu Wa-bohu)*, 2018
Ink on gessoed canvas
50 × 50 inches

Detail following

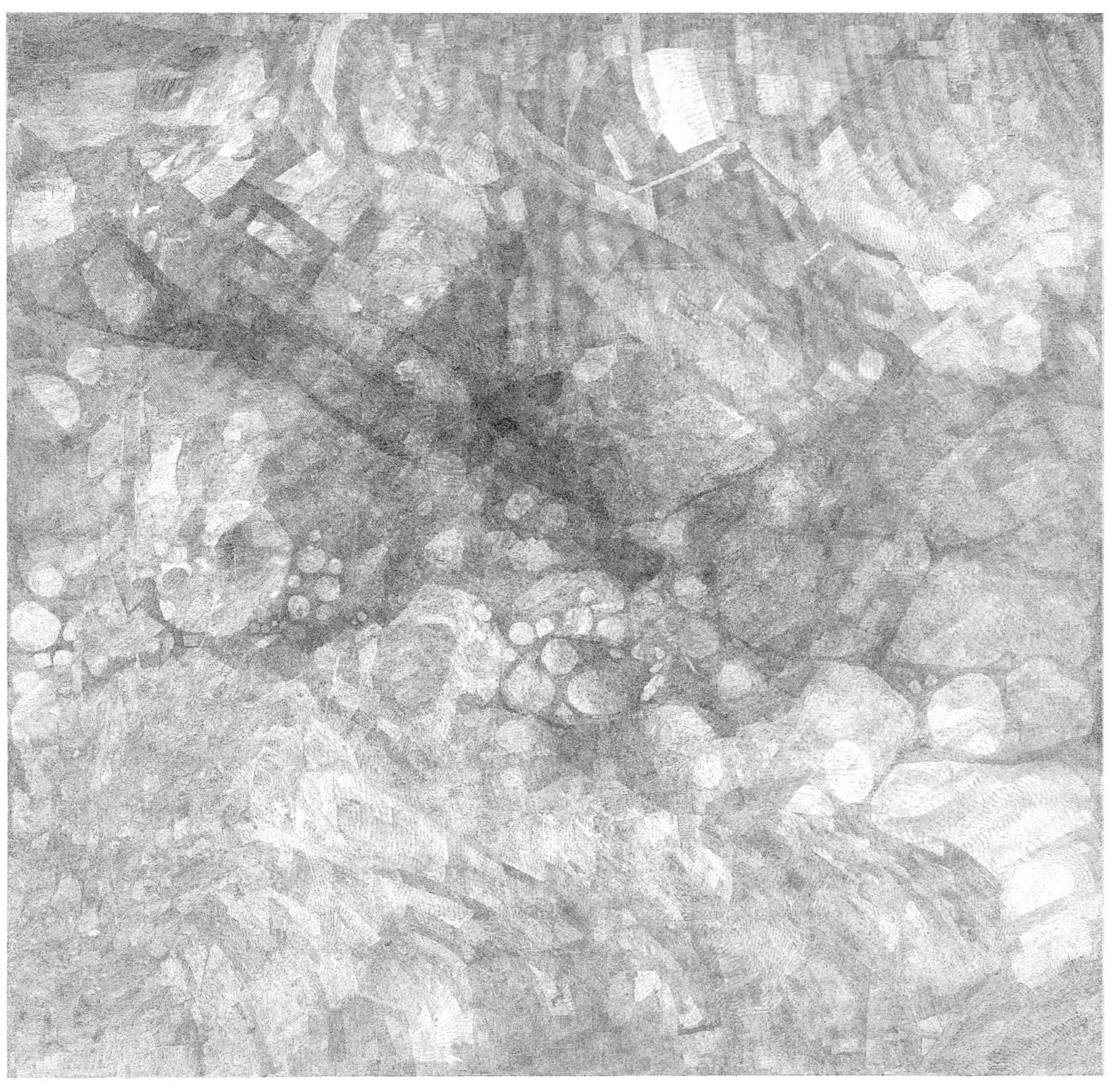

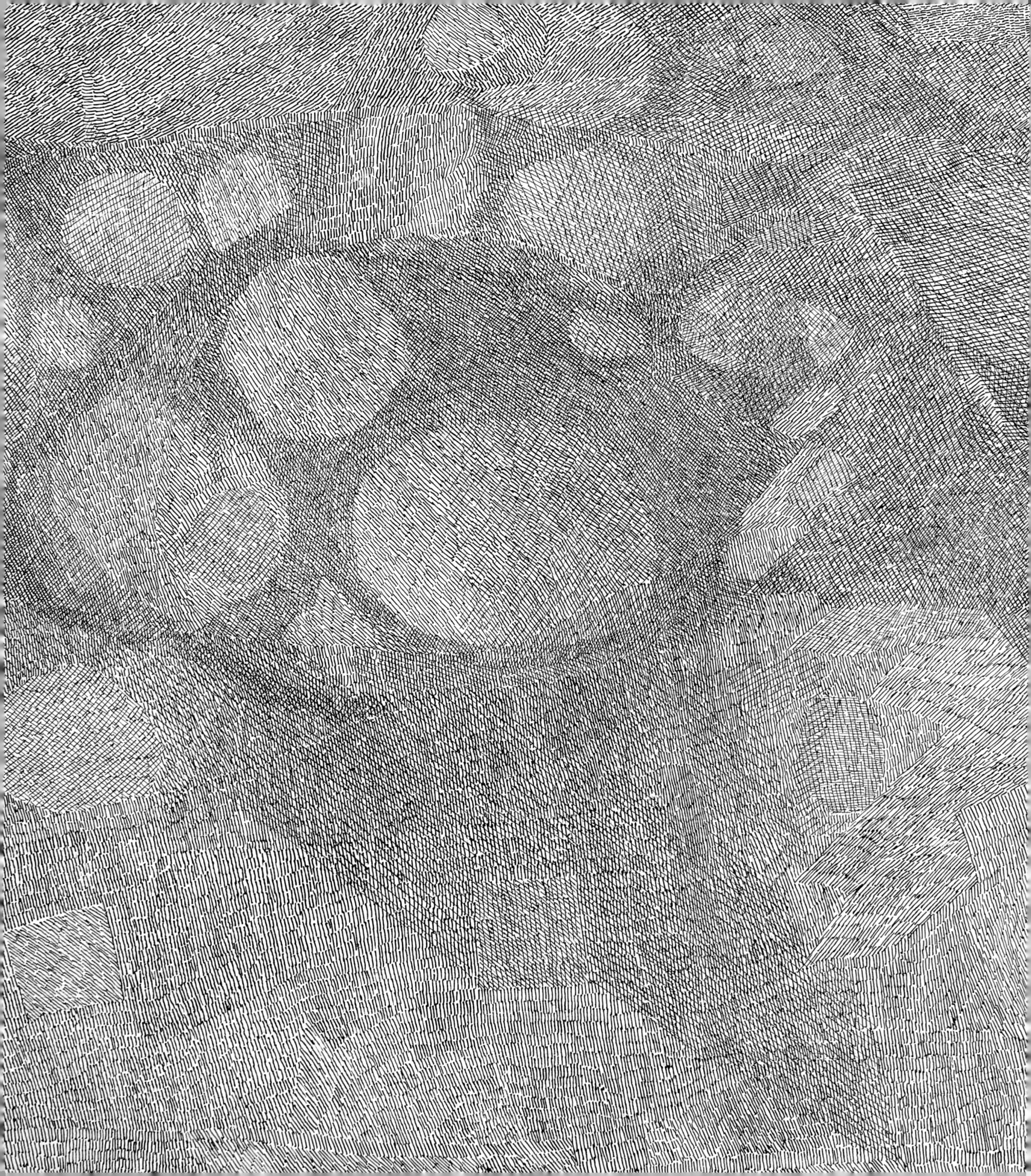

PLATE 12
Five Lines Basket, 2019
Ink on gessoed canvas
16 × 16 inches

Detail following

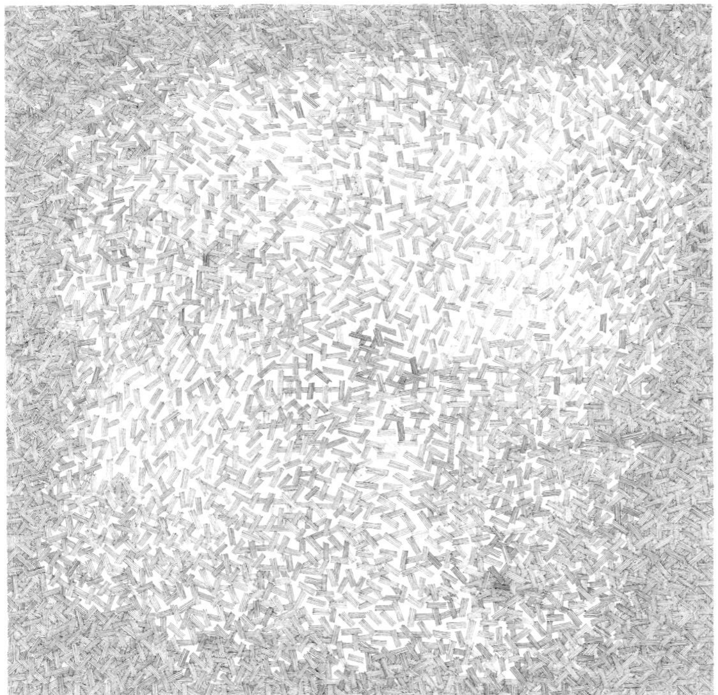

PLATE 13
Horizontal Line, 2018
Ink on gessoed canvas
20 × 24 inches

Detail following

PLATE 14
Lines Division, 2017
Ink on gessoed canvas
20 × 20 inches

Detail following

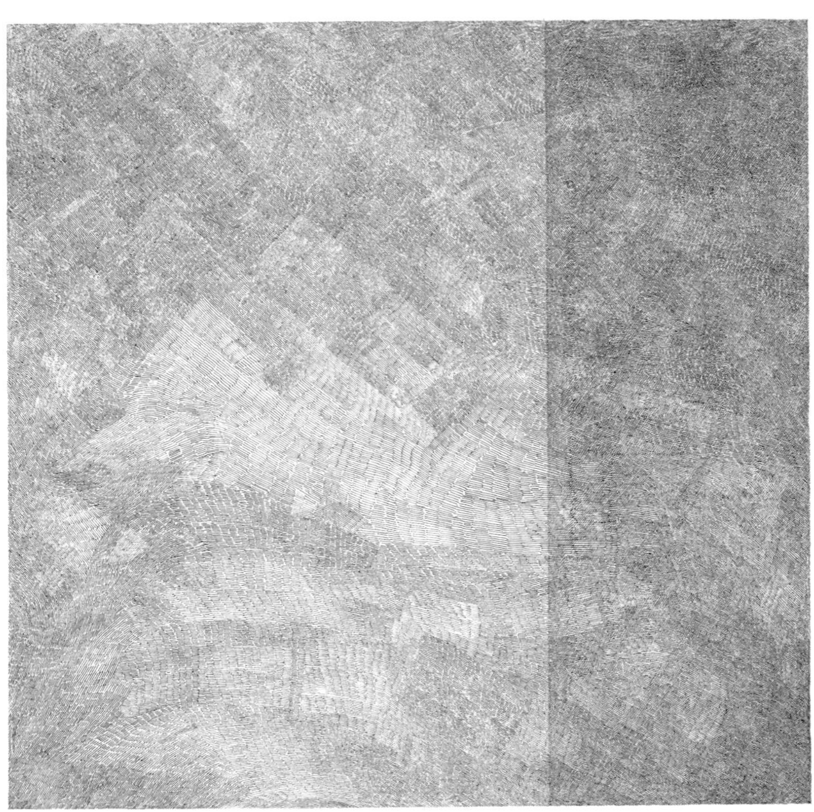

PLATE 15
IVRIT, 2020
Ink on gessoed canvas
10 × 10 inches

Detail following

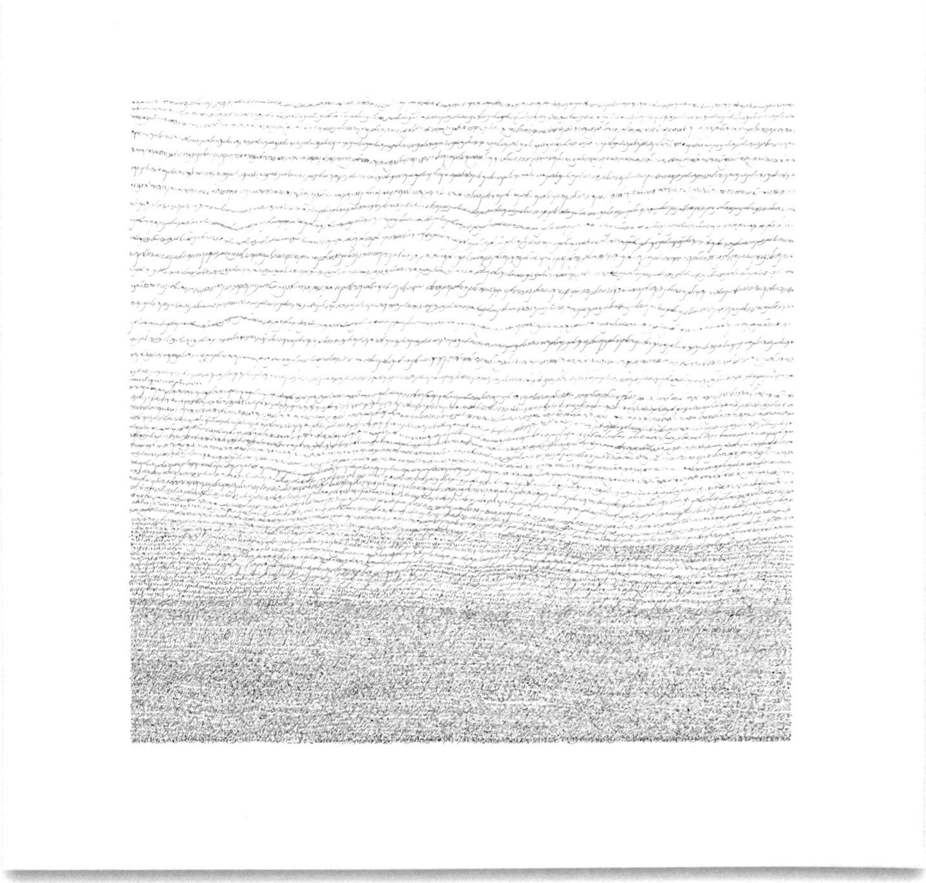

PLATE 16
Linen, 2020
Ink on gessoed canvas
10 × 10 inches

Detail following

PLATE 17
Broken Lines, 2019
Ink on gessoed canvas
10 × 10 inches

Detail following

PLATE 18
Crosshatch Forms, 2019
Ink on gessoed canvas
10 × 10 inches

Detail following

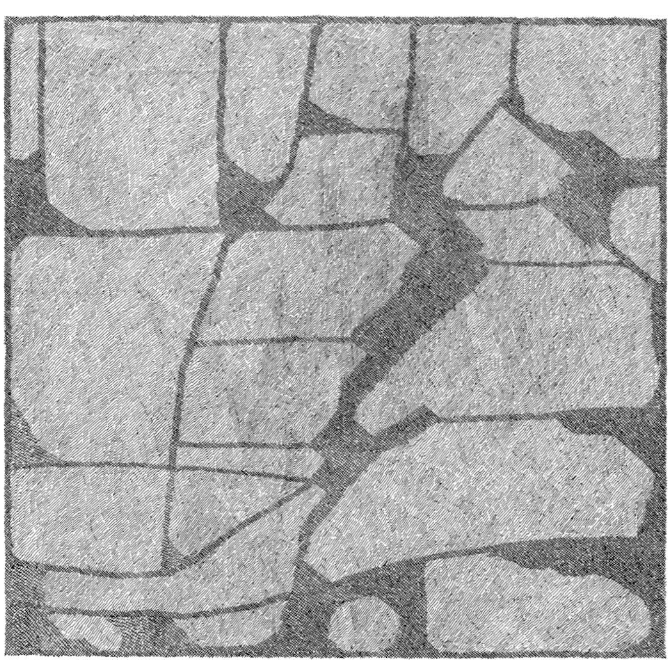

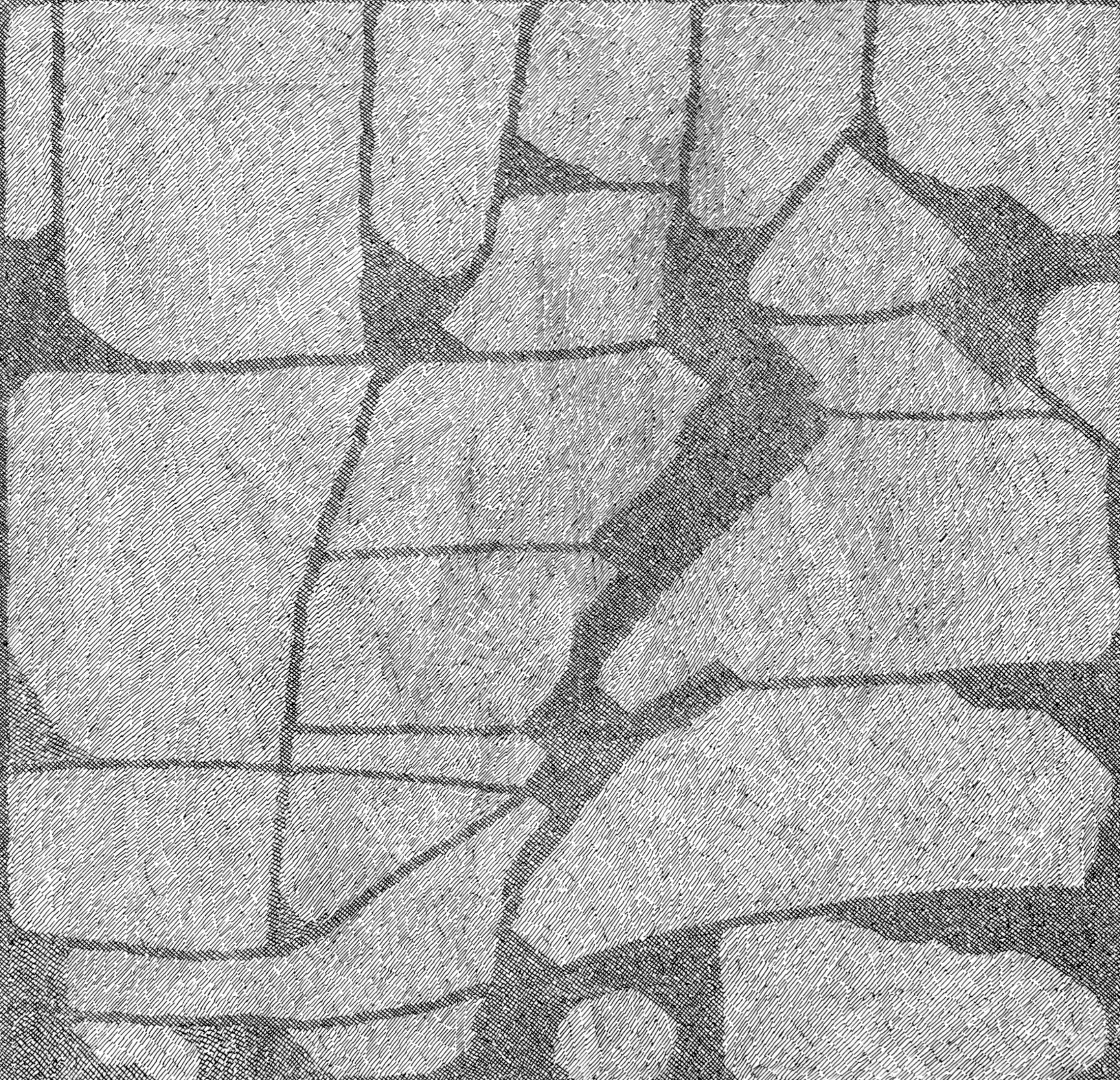

PLATE 19
Seven Line Open Basket, 2020
Ink on gessoed canvas
10 × 10 inches

Detail following

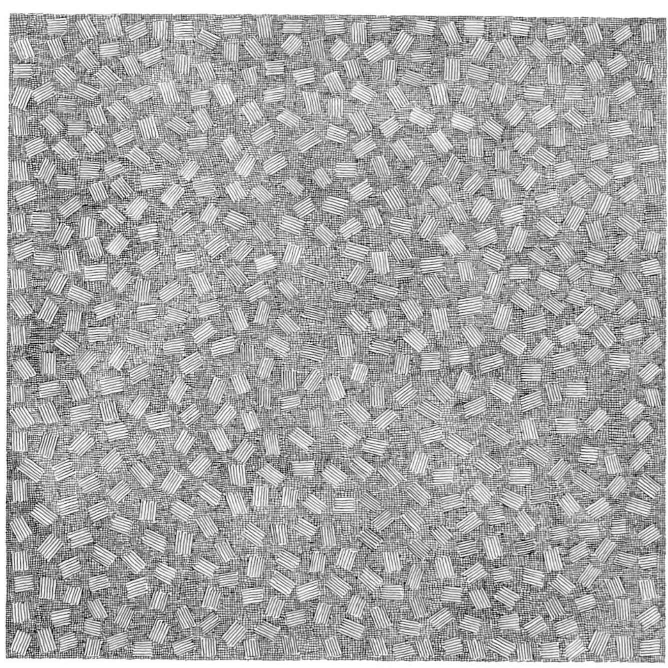

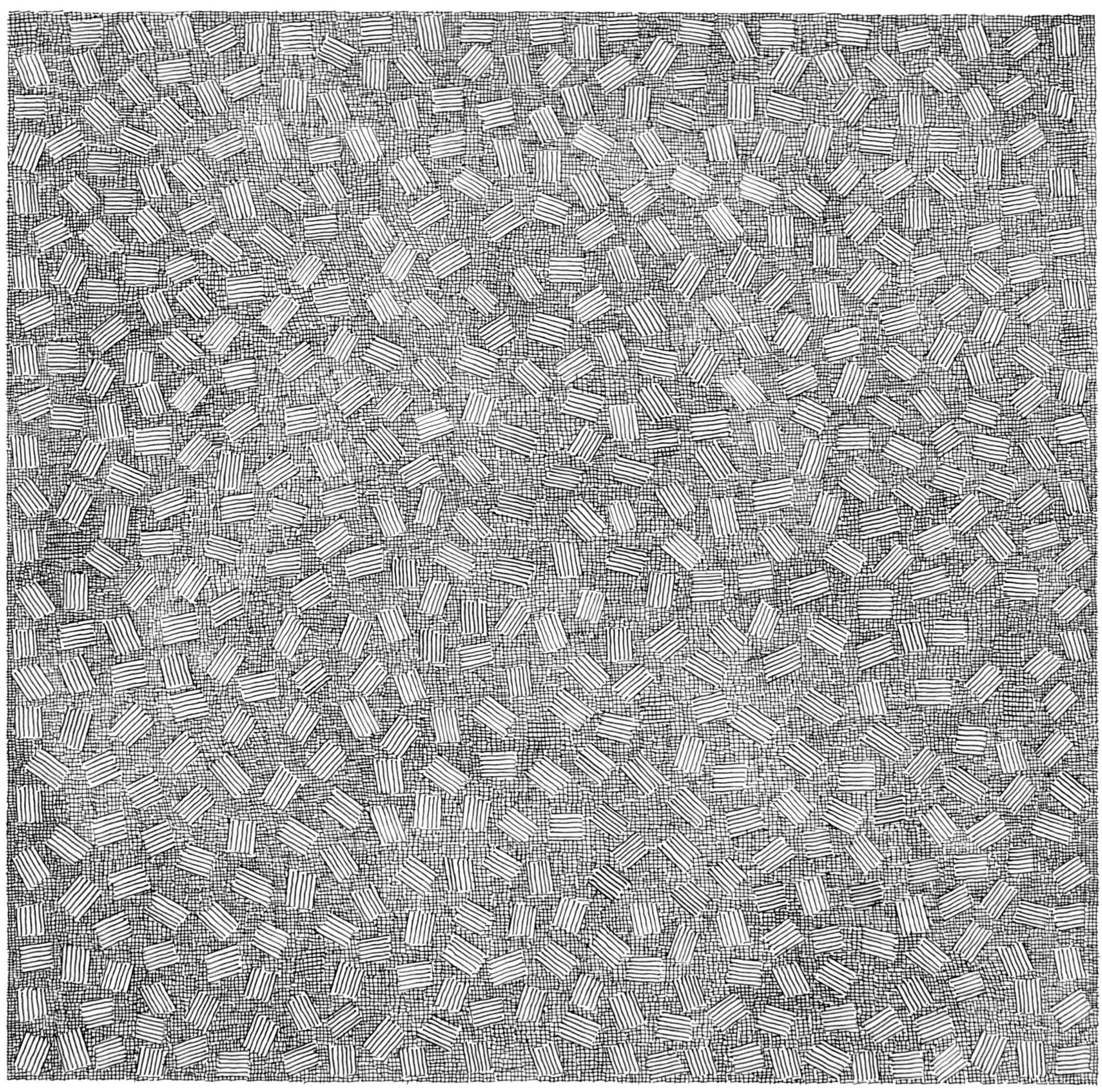

PLATE 20
Circle and Linescape, 2018
Ink on gessoed canvas
22 × 28 inches

Detail following

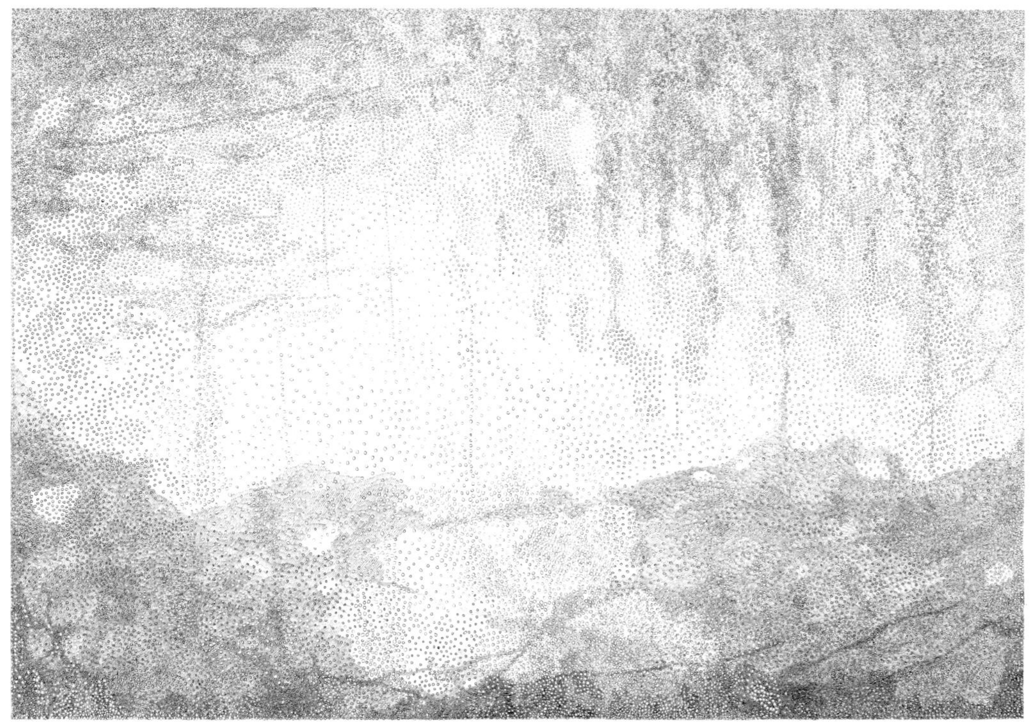

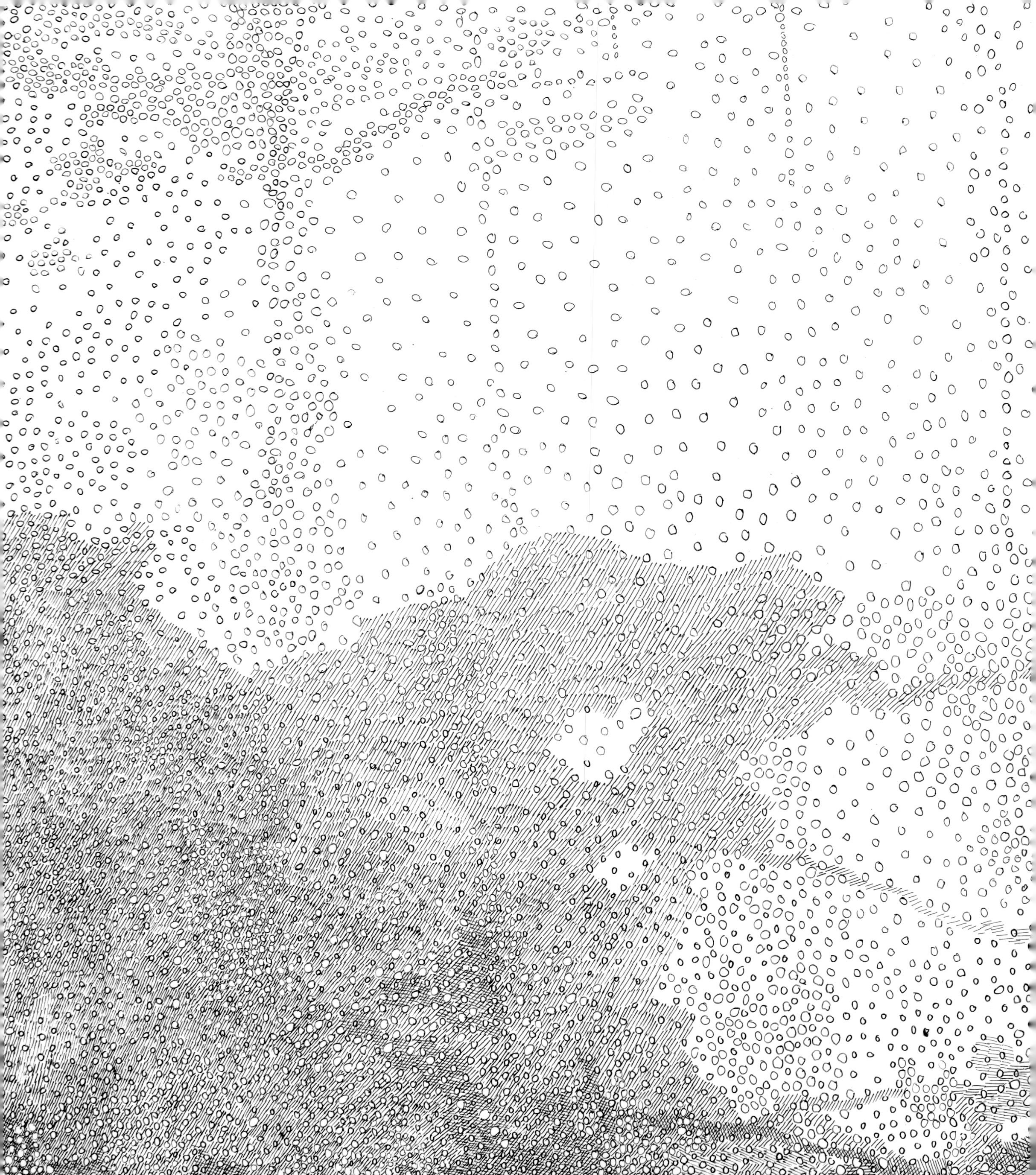

PLATE 21
Dot-Nekuda, 2019
Ink on gessoed canvas
36 × 36 inches

Detail following

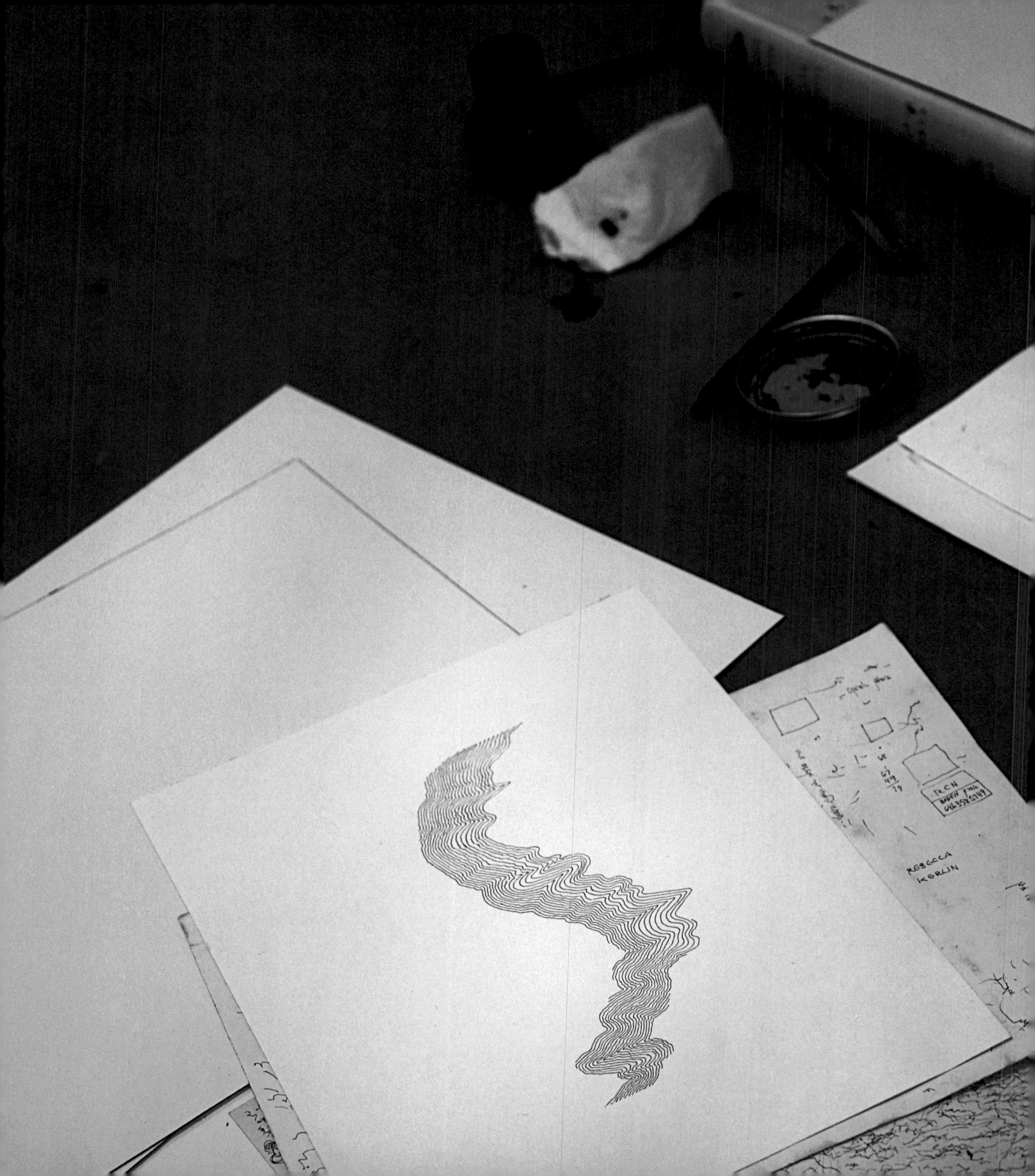
REBECCA
KERLIN

"These are not drawings that one can comprehend with a snapshot view; they require a commitment of time and attention simply to be seen, let alone understood. They insist on a unique protocol of viewing in which the usual strategies of positioning and time spent looking are useless. This is slow art at its purest, as slow in its making as in its viewing. But be forewarned, beneath this appearance of patience, beneath this modesty of means, beneath this partisanship with the diminutive lies a grand artistic ambition, a major achievement."

—RAPHAEL RUBINSTEIN

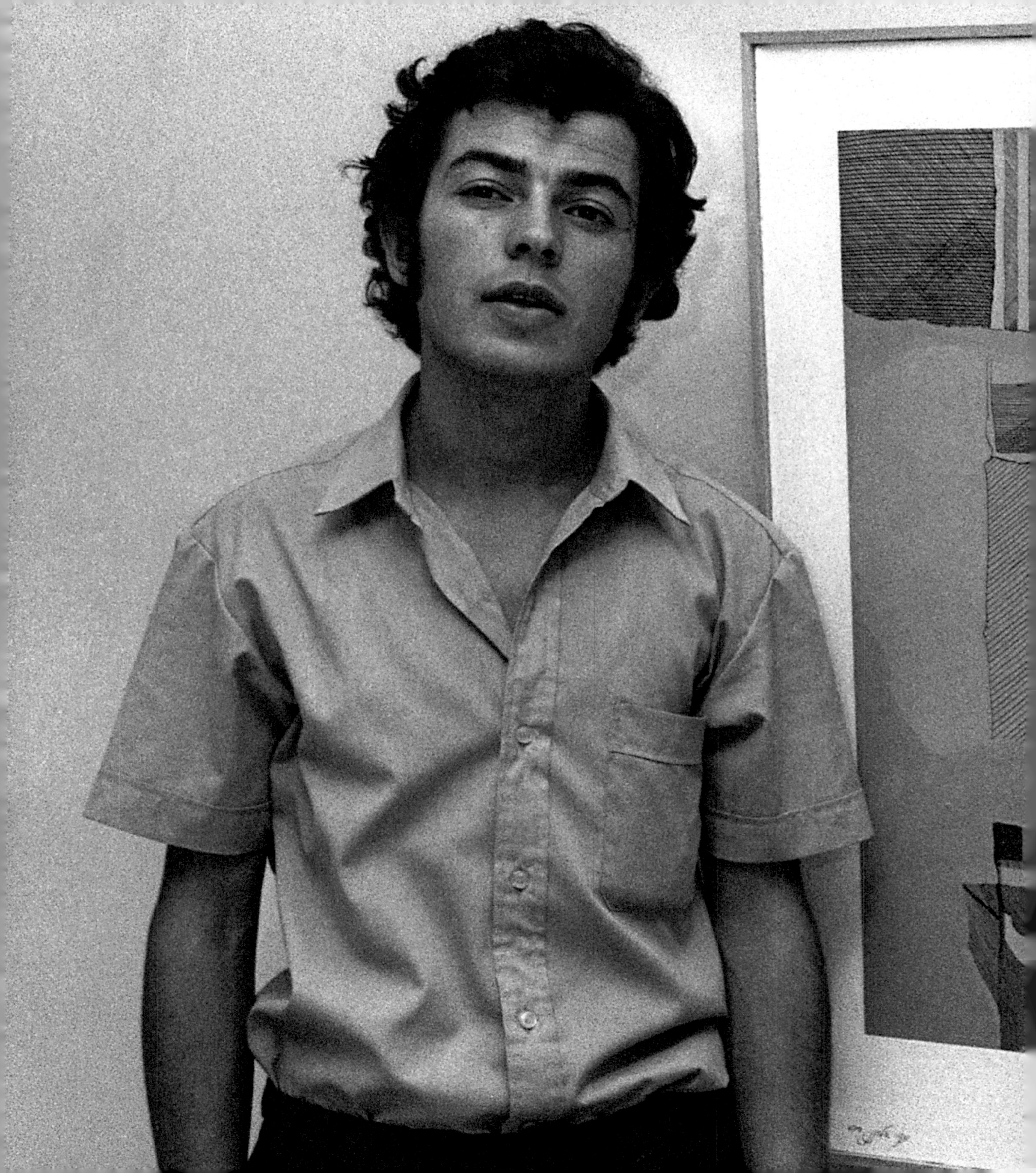

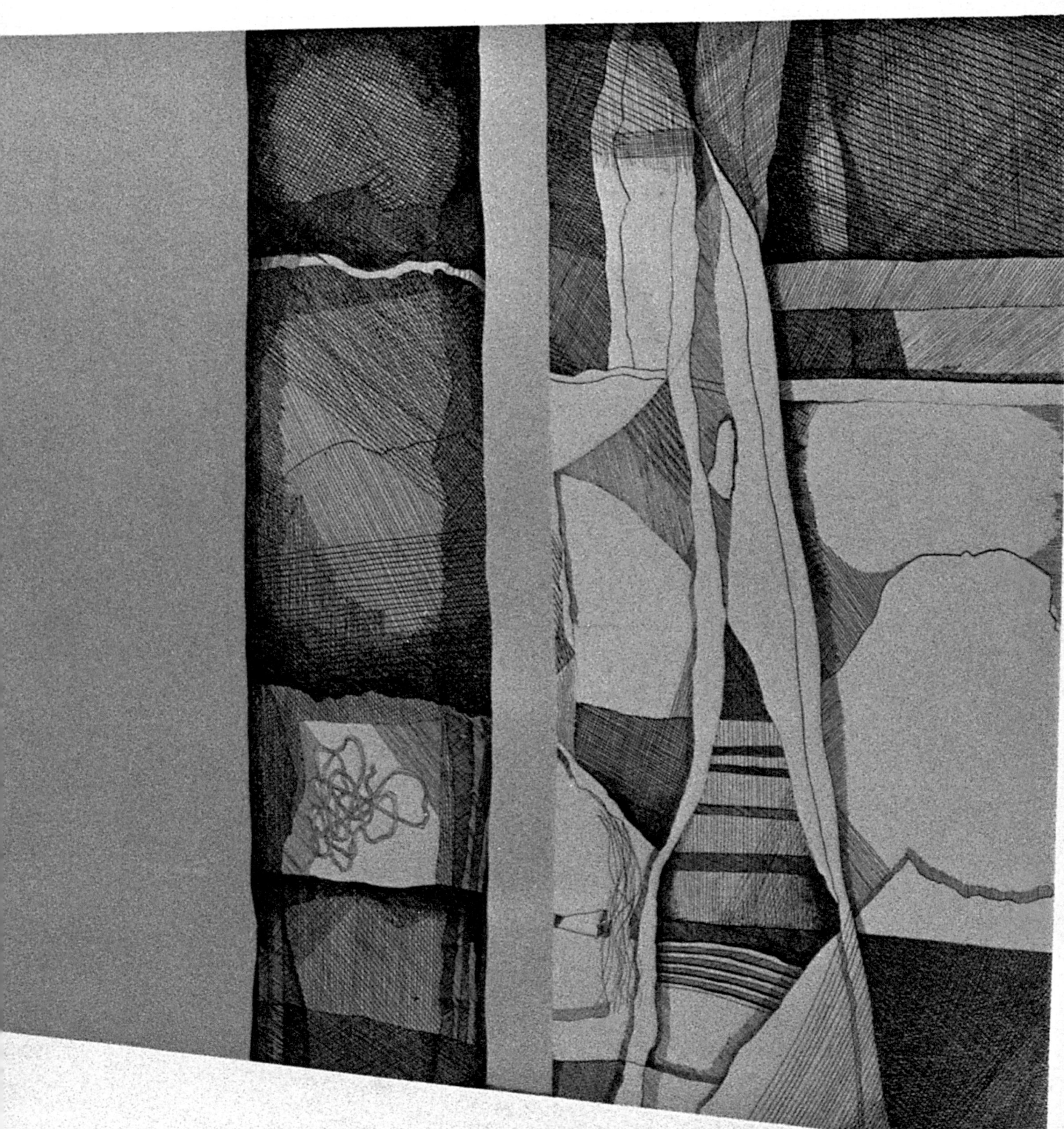

SOLO EXHIBITIONS

2017	*Jacob EL Hanani: Linescape*, Acquavella Galleries, NY
2015	*Jacob El Hanani Drawings*, Acquavella Galleries, NY
2014	*The Art of the Line*, Sammer Gallery LLC, Miami, FL
2012	*Linear Landscape: Ink Drawings*, Holly Johnson Gallery, Dallas, TX
2008	*Recent Work*, Steven Zevitas Gallery, Boston, MA
2005	*Drawing 1978–2005*, Mills College, Oakland, CA
2004	*Jacob El Hanani Drawings 1971–1987*, Gallery Schlesinger, New York, NY
2003	OSP Gallery, Boston, MA
2002	Nicole Klagsbrun Gallery, New York, NY
	Gallery Joe, Philadelphia, PA
2000	Mark Moore Gallery, Santa Monica, CA
	Nicole Klagsbrun Gallery, New York, NY
	Gallery Joe, Philadelphia, PA
1999	Miller/Block Gallery, Boston, MA
1998	Todd Hosfelt Gallery, San Francisco, CA
1995	Yoshii Gallery, New York, NY
1993	Galerie Renee Ziegler, Zurich
1988	Galerie Gilbert Brownstone, Paris
1978	Galerie Denise René, Paris
1977	Galerie Denise René, New York, NY
1975	Galerie Denise René, Paris

PREVIOUS SPREAD
Jacob El Hanani at Yad Labanim Gallery in Petah Tikva, Israel, July 1969

SELECTED COLLECTIONS
In order of acquisition

The Solomon R. Guggenheim Museum, New York

The Museum of Modern Art, New York

The Jewish Museum, New York

The Brooklyn Museum, New York

Musée National d'Art Moderne, Centre Georges Pompidou, Paris

The Israel Museum, Jerusalem

Art Gallery of Ontario, Toronto

The Menil Collection, Houston

The Metropolitan Museum of Art, New York

The Philadelphia Museum of Art, Philadelphia

The Hirshhorn Museum and Sculpture Garden, Smithsonian Institution, Washington, D.C.

The Art Institute of Chicago

Walker Art Center, Minneapolis

The Tel-Aviv Museum of Art, Tel Aviv

Petah Tikva Museum of Art, Petah Tikva

The National Gallery of Art, Washington, D.C.

Museo de Arte Contemporáneo de Caracas, Caracas

The Rose Art Museum, Brandeis University, Waltham

Minneapolis Institute of Arts, Mineeapolis

Yale University Art Gallery, New Haven

The Museum of Fine Arts, Houston

The Museum of Fine Arts, Boston

The Fogg Art Museum, Harvard University Art Museums, Cambridge

Cantor Arts Center at Stanford University, Stanford, California

Weatherspoon Art Museum, University of North Carolina at Greensboro, Greensboro

Neuberger Museum of Art, Purchase College State University of New York, Purchase

The British Museum, London

Minneapolis Institute of Arts, Minneapolis

The Whitney Museum of American Art, New York

The Morgan Library & Museum, New York

Pérez Art Museum Miami, Miami

Memorial Art Gallery, University of Rochester, Rochester

Pennsylvania Academy of the Fine Arts, Philadelphia

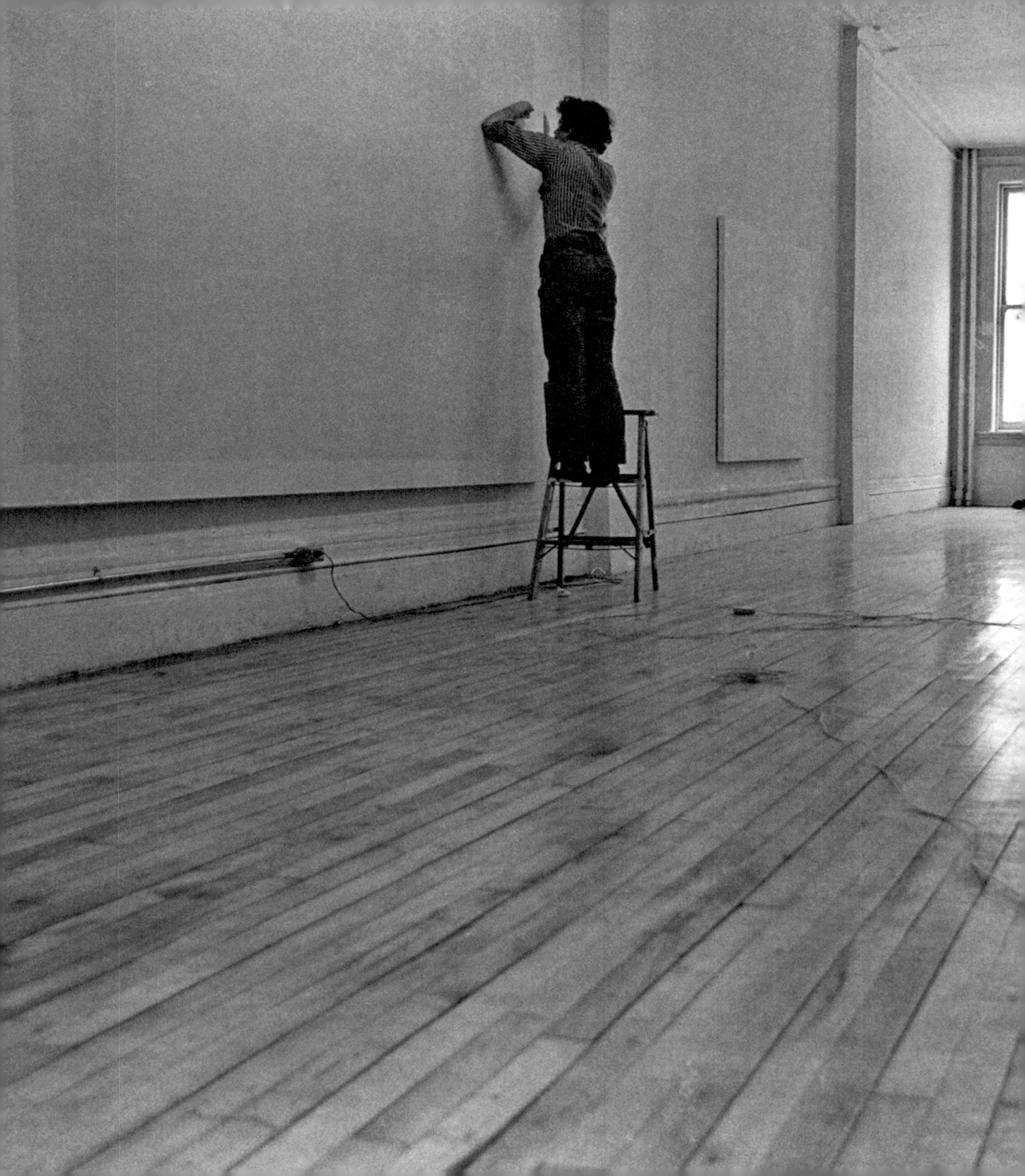

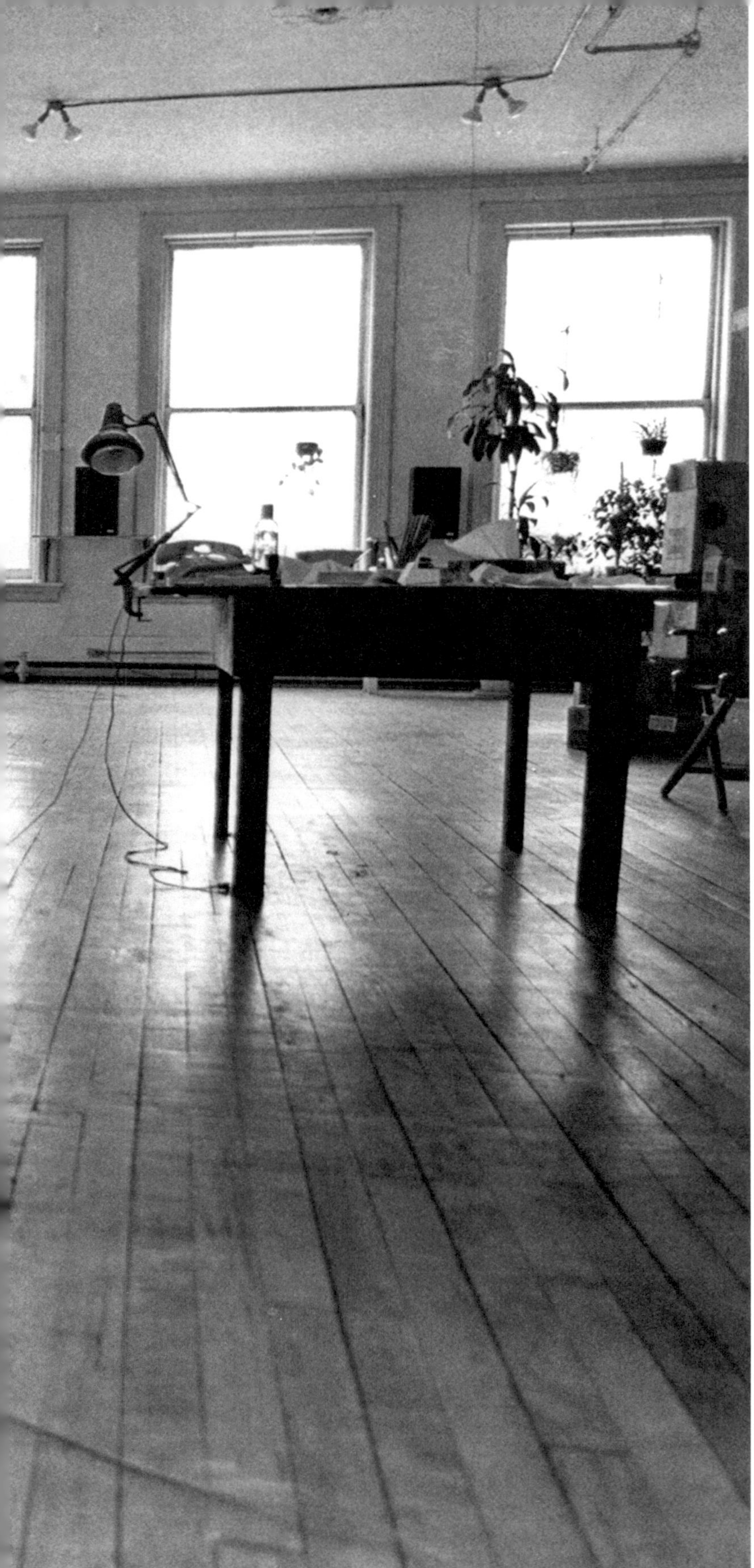

Jacob El Hanani in his studio
in Soho, New York, 1974

AUTHOR'S BIOGRAPHY

Adam Kirsch is a poet and critic whose books include *The People and the Books: 18 Classics of Jewish Literature* and *Rocket and Lightship: Essays on Literature and Ideas.* He is a regular contributor to *The New Yorker, The New York Review of Books*, and other publications.

IMAGE CREDITS

Unless otherwise noted, all photos of works of art by Jacob El Hanani are by Kent Pell.

PAGE 7
Detail of Plate 3: *The Horizontal Hebrew Alphabet*, 2019.

PAGES 8, 112
Photos by Allison Carey, 2020.

PAGE 17
Image source: Art Resource, NY.

PAGE 18
Art © 1998 Kate Rothko Prizel & Christopher Rothko / Artists Rights Society (ARS), New York.

PAGE 20
Image courtesy The British Library.

PAGE 25
Works by Park Seo-Bo, Chryssa, Jacob El Hanani, Brice Marden, Roman Opalka and Zarina on view, left to right. Photo by David Heald. Art by Brice Marden is © 2021 Brice Marden/Artists Rights Society (ARS), New York. Art by Roman Opalka is © 2021 Artists Rights Society (ARS), New York / ADAGP, Paris.

PAGES 114–15, 117
Images courtesy the artist.